Passive Income 2021: For Beginners. Learn
strategies and psychology to Earn money
with Social Media in 2021 and Beyond

Copyright © 2020

Table of Contents

Introduction

This guidebook is meant to help the reader get the most out of several passive income sources that can be utilized these days. Many individuals are interested in getting a passive income going. They love dreaming about living on the beach and traveling to vacation hotspots in Gulfstream jets or yachts, doing anything they want to do at all times. But only a few realize the hard work that must go into creating a passive stream of income. The effort will be compounded if you must create several streams of passive income.

In this book, you will learn some of the numerous and different steps you may need to take in order to earn the best passive income possible. There are several options that you can choose from when it comes to earning income passively. But that can only be possible if you take certain steps that ensure you become very successful with it.

Therefore, in order to make the most out of this book, follow the steps outlined below:

1. Figure out what source of passive income you love and will be interested in working with. This will open your eyes in

order to know the direction you should follow with the steps outlined in this book.

2. Work through each of these steps slowly, one at a time. This will make it far easier for you to give each step the attention and time it needs instead of rushing through them.

3. Whatever advice you come across in this book, it is highly recommended that you take it seriously, not with a pinch of salt. It is essential that you work with each step in order to see the results you seek or want. Too many individuals have rushed through the processes of creating passive income, hoping to start making money within a few weeks. The steps outlined in this book will show you how to get it done.

4. Put everything together and be ready to put in some hard work and dedication. You will eventually be able to start earning the passive income that you have been dreaming about, which will remain elusive to many.

Although many people today want to earn their own passive income, it can be hard to work with. You will never be able to make any passive income if you don't put in any work or within a few weeks.

But with the tips that will be shared in this book, you will be able to earn this kind of income and enjoy success within a short period.

Chapter One

What is Passive Income?

Many people have heard of the words 'Passive income,' but only a few are curious enough to explore further. And sadly, even those who know what passive income is and how it can dramatically change their lives for the better will never experience it. Yes, they do love the idea of making a side income as a result of a side hustle while retaining their regular 9-5 jobs. Many even fantasize about going on vacations in the Bahamas or the Cayman Islands and generally enjoying life.

A lot comes with having a passive income because it is not just something that you turn your attention to when you feel like it. The truth of the matter is that you will need to work hard at first before the going becomes good, and that is if you have taken the right steps or done the right things. Over time, that hard work you put in when you started the journey will begin to pay off, and for many years to come, fetching you a good income weekly or monthly.

Therefore, what do you need to know about passive income? Here's what you need to know about creating a passive income and what it entails to build businesses that generate passive income

What is passive income?

Passive income can be a form of earning money that anyone can get and from any endeavor. It could be from a rental property or something else that does not require your active involvement day in, day out.

Passive income is taxable, just like regular active income, in the United States. However, the IRS treats this type of income a bit differently than other types of income. Nevertheless, it is an excellent way to make some income on real estate, investments as well as other kinds of endeavors without the need for you to have a direct relationship with each day.

To get a better understanding of passive income, it is essential to, first of all, take a look at the major types of income that are presently available. There are 3 of these that you can focus on building: portfolio income, active income, and passive income.

Passive income is a term that has changed a lot over the past few years. The way most people see it these days is far different from how it was in the past, which is a good thing. All that is required now is to learn more about it as much as you can, as well as how this kind of income works so that you can apply all you learn to make it work for you.

As a rule, a passive income is used to define any money you earn on a regular basis with very little – and sometimes – no effort on your part. It does sound like a dream come true; who wouldn't want to sit back and relax without having to do anything, yet money keeps trickling into your bank account.

There are different types of passive income that you can work with. The most popular or common options that are presently available include peer to peer, real estate, limited partnership, investing in dividend stocks, or any other enterprise.

If you see passive income as a good or positive thing, then you must be a booster of work at home. And you should be ready to lead a 'Be your own boss' kind of lifestyle. The types of earning you may earn at first may be small, but if you work hard, the income will eventually grow and become successful.

Why Should You Build Passive Income?

The greatest wealth-building tool is your income, which usually requires your active participation in the form of a full-time, 9-5 job.

No matter how much you earn, working your 9-5 job, you won't say "No" to make some extra side income without too much sweat, blood, and time commitment.

Several benefits are associated with earning income passively. When you build a passive income, it does the following:

- Boosts your wealth-building plan
- Protects you from a sudden and complete loss of income if you lose your job
- Creates a rare opportunity to retire early
- It provides another stream of income, especially when you can no longer hold down a 9-5 job or outlast your retirement fund.

How Much Money Can You Make Passively?

What you need to know straight away is that passive income will not make you wealthy overnight. So, get rid of any get-rich-quick schemes or thoughts that may be passing through your mind.

However, if you follow the highly profitable passive income options that will be outlined later on in this uique book, you will be able to build a lot of serious money in the long run. You could make any amount from a few hundred dollars to hundreds of thousands of dollars, depending on the stream of income you opt for.

Types of Passive Income

Here are the types of passive income you need to know:

-Property

Rental properties can be said to be passive income, though with a couple of exceptions. If you get involved in the real estate industry or become a professional in the industry, any rental income you make usually counts as an active income. If you own a space and rent it out to a partnership where you run your day-to-day business or corporation, it cannot be counted as a passive income source.

The only way it will count as passive income is if the lease was signed before 1988, which implies that you have virtually been grandfathered into having that income. According to the IRS Passive Activity and At-Risk Rules: 'It doesn't matter whether or not the use is under a service contract, a lease, or some other arrangement.'

Nevertheless, income generated from leasing land does not qualify as passive income. But then, as a landowner, you can benefit from passive income loss rules if that property nets a loss during the tax year. As for holding land for investment, all earnings are considered active.

-Self-charged interest

When money is loaned to an S-corporation or a partnership that acts as a pass-through entity – i.e., a business that is designed to minimize the effects of double taxation – by the entity's owner, the interest generated on that loan to the portfolio income qualifies as passive income.

Certain self-charged deductions or interest income may be treated as passive activity deductions or passive activity gross income if the loan proceeds are used in a passive activity.

'No Material Participation' in a Business

Let's say you put $200,000 into a candy store after having an agreement with the owners that they will pay you a percentage of earnings, it will be considered passive income. But only if you do not directly participate in running the business in any meaningful way apart from placing the investment. The IRS states that if you help in managing the organization with the owners, your income will be perceived as active because you offered 'material participation.'

The IRS has set standards for material participation that include:

- If you have participated in up to 100 hours, which is as much as any other individual involved in the activity, it may be defined as material participation.
- If you have dedicated over 500 hours to an activity or business from which you are profiting, that is referred to as material participation.
- If your participation in an activity or business has been 'substantially all' of the involvement within that tax year, it is known as material participation.

Chapter Two

The 7 Streams of Income of Most Millionaires

Are you one of the numerous individuals out there with only one stream of income? Do you even know the average millionaire has more than 3 streams of income? Perhaps, that explains why they got rich so fast while you are still grinding at your daily or regular 9-to-5 job, barely making enough before the next payday. There is a lot much money out there to be made, but if you are not doing the right things to channel the money your way, you will remain the way you are for many years to come.

So, how many streams of legitimate income are you even aware of? The internet is rife with lots of get-rich-quick hype and glorification on how to become an overnight millionaire. But the truth is that many lots of people have grown comfortable living average lifestyles. Many have resigned to living mediocre lives, with no desire or drive to earn a great deal of money than they need to live fairly comfortably. It seems most people want to stop trading time for money or minimize the time they spend making some money.

To live comfortably holds different meanings to different people; some believe that living comfortably means they earn enough to get by, while others believe that becoming a millionaire is the only guarantee to live comfortably.

However, one thing that most people have, whether they were born with silver spoons – or wooden spoons as the case may be – is time. And every one goes through life trying to balance the time spent with family, the time spent working, and other aspects of life.

Here are the 7 income streams of millionaires:

1.   Earned income

This is the money you earn when you spend your time or do something, i.e., the money you make in your day-to-day job, the salary you are paid when you work for an organization or someone.

This is where the quality of most salary earners suffers the most since they trade time for money. Jobs, in most cases, pay you just enough to stay above the 'broke' level. Perhaps that is why someone somewhere took every letter of the word 'job' and turned it into an acronym for 'Just Over Broke.'

The primary reason why most people hold down jobs is that they do not want to think beyond making money by trading their time because a job provides them with a reasonably comfortable income or zone. They love to remain in this comfort zone with the promise of earning some money when they reach their golden years.

But the problem with such a comfort zone is that it becomes your greatest enemy and will prevent you from reaching for an extraordinary life. The world is your oyster, but you may spend the productive years of your life in this income category. And you may never have enough money to lead a wealthy and extraordinary life.

If you can only come out from your comfort zone, defeating your life's biggest enemy, your life will improve drastically.

2. Interest income

This is the money you earn as a result of lending your money to a friend or colleague. For example, the extra money you make when you put your money in a bank, lend a colleague to launch a thriving business or government for purchasing Treasury Bills, etc. are interest income.

This is a great and excelent source of passive income in which your active involvement is not required as soon as the investment is made. Despite this, however, many people seriously doubt the efficacy of 'Interest Income' and its potential to generate wealth.

But its actual effect is felt when you consider the power of compounding. This is the perfect example of passive income as it involves minimum risk and even beats some of the income streams of most millionaires on this list hands down.

3. Profit income

This is the money you earn when you sell a product or item for more than it costs you to make or produce. For instance, most brick-and-mortar businesses sell products at a profit, at the wholesale or retail level. Manufacturers and distributors do the same thing. If you must earn profits, then you need to be an entrepreneur.

To start earning profit income, you may need a considerable investment as a start or launch a small business with a small investment. However, this could eat into your time, at least when you are still in the initial stages. But if you keep at it and learn to manage it incredibly well by automating some aspects of it, you will start earning remarkable profits. Entrepreneurship requires a different kind of mindset, which is not the same as those who love earned income via salaries, and so on.

Most people who are used to earning salaries usually find it pretty difficult to make a move to entrepreneurship, even if they want to at any stage of their illustrious career or life. The primary reason for this is the lack the courage to step out of their comfort zones and take steps into unchartered waters. And in most cases, this lack of guts may be relatively justified because of the family's needs and constraints.

To be a very successful entrepreneur, one who starts earning steady profits, the first thing you should do is identify a product or service. This product or service should be sellable, and you should be able to manage it as well as your clients.

Many people limit themselves to the 'Earned Income' and 'Profit Income' levels all their lives, forgetting that there are other serious ways of making money legitimately.

4. Dividend income

This is another stream of income that you should consider. Dividend Income is equally passive, and the additional benefit is that you will become a shareholder of an organization. This is the money you receive as a return or income on shares of an organization you own.

A perfect example is a dividend that most organizations announce or declare at the end of every year. Despite the efficacy of dividend income, many people today ignore this highly lucrative stream of income.

Take steps to invest smartly on the ex-dividend dates of highly successful blue-chip companies. The amount of money you will earn annually will far exceed that of 'Interest Income,' especially since you are now party to the Capital Gains that the share price undergoes. Therefore, it is one of the vital instruments that is highly recommended by millionaires for generating adequate and steady Cash Flow while getting a very good income.

5.   Rental income

This is the money you make when you rent out an asset that belongs to you, such as a house or an entire building. This source of income is far better than others on this list, though there are a few drawbacks that must be mentioned.

First of all, the biggest drawback of this type of income is the amount of money required to purchase or create such an asset that will generate consistent rental income. The hugeness of that amount of money can make it impossible for you to develop or have such assets throughout your lifetime. The only way this could be possible, especially if you always limit yourself to the 'Earned Income' level, is to have other trusted sources of regular income.

For instance, you can start earning 'Dividend Income' or 'Income Interest' with an investment that starts from $500 or more. And when compound interest sets in, you are on your way to earning rental income with careful management on your part.

Another drawback has to do with the liquidity of the asset. It is often difficult to liquefy assets that generate Rental income quickly, especially when you move or change residence or in times of need or balance your portfolio mix.

6. Capital Gains

This is the money you receive when an asset that you own increases in value. For instance, when you purchase shares at $10 and sell it off at $12, the $2 is referred to as capital gains. The same can be applied when you buy a house at $150,000 and sell it for $200,000; the $20,000 is your capital gains.

Every country has different tax laws on capital gains, and you can even learn ways to come around taxes when the time comes.

7. Royalty income

You can only get this type of income when you allow someone else to use your ideas, products, or processes. That person makes all the revenue as well as all the hard work while you sit back and receive a small percentage of whatever that person earns.

For instance, let's say you have McDonald's Franchise; the royalty you sent to McDonald's for using their logo, marketing, processes, etc. is royalty income for them. If you write and sell books, you will get paid for every copy of the book that is sold.

The biggest challenge you may encounter or face when trying to get into this income level is to create something exceptionally unique and then make it repeatable. This will require special skills in order to create such an asset.

But the beautiful thing is that as soon as you create that asset, there is practically no limit to the amount of money that you can make or earn.

These are the 7 streams of income of most millionaires you see today. This is not to imply that all millionaires must have all of these 7 income streams. For instance, Warren Buffet is the billionaire that was quoted as saying, 'If you do not find a way to make money while you sleep, you will work all the days of your life.' Despite his status, he does not make most of his money from all the 7 streams of income outlined in this chapter. Buffet became a millionaire via Capital Gains and Dividend Income.

However, he did not get into Capital Gains on everything; in fact, he specialized in a tiny aspect, which is Capital Gains of organizations in the stock market. Then he honed his skills continually, year in, year out in valuing companies and re-investing in them until he eventually became a millionaire, and then a billionaire.

Bill Gates, who was once, the wealthiest individual in the world, generated most of his income via 'Royalty Income' and 'Profit Income.' The billionaire created an organization as well as an asset known as 'Windows.' He used the asset to change the way everyone interacts with computers today. Gates became so good by earning stupendous amounts of money through the income models discussed earlier. He climbed up the charts, appearing in Forbes magazine as one of the wealthiest individuals in the world.

There are several millionaires out there today who earned that status via the 'Profit Income' model. But then, they were pretty good at whatever it was they were doing. Perform enough research online, and you will come across individuals who became millionaires from Royalty Income.

Therefore, start paying more attention to what you can do right now from at least one of these streams of income outlined in this chapter. And from there, start taking steps to become the best you can be in a small but profitable niche.

'Earned Income' involves trading time for money, and this puts a severe limit on the amount of money you can make since there is a limit to the number of hours you can put in a day. All other income streams are not dependent on time; therefore, you can leverage time exceptionally well to generate wealth.

So, take enough time to choose your streams. You will be taking a substantial financial risk if you depend on only one source of income where you need to be actively involved. Get more details about each income stream so that you can understand them even more. Then take steps to try them out. This could be one of the most life-changing or earth-shaking decisions you could make, which will affect not only you but also generations after you.

Chapter Three

Top 20 Best Future Business Ideas for 2020-2030

The future that we craved for many years ago is here, and the future that is to come will be created by our actions today.

Therefore if you really want to jump on the bandwagon and create businesses that will practically outlive you, the best time to start is now. You should know that small businesses are not going anywhere anytime soon and the same can be said of the internet.

Online marketing is getting set to become the most important thing for small businesses from 2020 to 2030. There are presently about 30 million small businesses in the United States alone. But that is not an indication that you shouldn't create yours because there is always space for more companies that offer value to its target market.

So, here are the top 55 best future business ideas for 2020 to 2030:

1. Internet Infrastructure

Businesses are presently restructuring and have increased their online interactions. And this massive reconstruction has created a growing need for advanced internet structure.

Internet infrastructure is projected to see an incredibly massive growth of 2.2 percent from 2020 to 2025. The expected generated revenue of this enormous business opportunity will be more than $37 million by the end of 2020.

Internet infrastructure connects internet users and allows them to interact with anyone in the world. Organizations are always looking for feasible solutions to deal with their internet demands and operate what is known as 'high-capacity backbones.'

High–capacity backbones are the process of connecting NAP (Network Access Protection) on a universal scale. This means that business owners can control the overall health of their computers and associated policies.

Here are several benefits for any business that chooses its own internet infrastructure:

- Security

- Efficient and scalable

- Location independence

- Cost-effective

More businesses will undoubtedly carry out daily transactions on the internet, thereby driving the demand for an effective and affordable solution like this one.

2. Amazon FBA Business

Amazon FBA (Fulfillment by Amazon) allows everyday people to source several physical products abroad and launch your unique brand. And the lovely thing about FBA is that you do not have to maintain inventory, deal or ship with returns yourself.

One common thing that FBA sellers do is to load up extra bonuses/items onto a suitable product in a bid to add even more value. For instance, selling a zucchini spiral spaghetti maker makes a lot of sense. However, you can add more value by adding a few cookbooks along with a skin peeler.

Building this business requires perseverance and a lot of patience. The primary factor that determines success is the product you pick. If you choose a product you don't connect with, you can quickly liquid your inventory by running paid Google or Facebook ads in order to recover your inventory expenses.

And as soon as the product ranks high on search engines and starts receiving a decent amount of good reviews from happy and satisfied customers, you have successfully built for yourself a piece of property on the web that will keep generating passive income for you for life which is a pretty good feeling.

The truth is that there are several moving parts to this business that you have to master. So, search for and invest in a good course that will show you how to go about it.

3. Chatbots

Chatbots are the rave of the moment nowadays, and that is because many organizations utilize them to handle minor customer service interactions personally and quickly. Research has shown that the outlook of these mini assistants is expected to reach a 136 percent growth rate over the next eighteen months.

You can invest in the design and implementation of a Chabot. It is imperative to hit up the perfect clientele to get optimal cash for your hard work. Therefore, you can readily get in touch with the following companies in order to get a high ROI on your investment:

- Bloggers
- Marketing agencies
- Gyms and fitness centers
- Authors
- Realtors
- Insurance agencies

Chatbots are potential passive income generators if you know what you are doing.

4. Drones

Starting a drone business is now more viable than ever, especially due to the many uses for drones in today's fast-paced market. Several industries use drones so much that researchers have projected the drone industry to be worth more than $100 billion by the end of 2020.

A variety of different models and prices exist today, which small businesses can capitalize on in order to create a nice stockpile of drones for use. Drones can be used for the following:

- Security
- Agriculture
- Search and rescue
- Surveying land

Corporations and governments continue to explore numerous ways to capture vital data and footage using drones.

5. Create an Online Course

Creating an online course is another digital product that has the potential to generate a steady stream of passive income. If you are an expert or possess a marketable skill, you can create a series of audio recordings or videos to impart your knowledge.

You may prefer to create eBooks, though this requires a lot of work upfront, especially if you are not conversant with creating courses.

But if you eventually do, eBooks that get updated from time to time can turn to a profitable avenue for passive income.

There are several online platforms for course creators to use, such as Teachable, Udemy, Google Open Online Education, and Thinkific. There are profitable markets for different kinds of courses, from how to code to how to perform strength exercises.

Most people have skills and knowledge which they can turn into a course. But the #1 challenge centers more on finding the energy and time to start and finish creating the course and attracting the right audience or customers who will purchase the course.

6. Virtual Medical Appointment System

Do you know that the healthcare system – as a whole – has lost more than $150 billion within a calendar year as a result of appointment no-shows. You can imagine the devastating impact on independent clinics and hospitals.

You can fill this void by developing an interactive, affordable, and reliable online medical appointment system that can help these small clinics and hospitals fine-tune their patient notification and follow-up processes.

This is an extraordinary innovation that is incredibly high in demand and will continue to expand as the new decade progresses.

7.   Biometric Sensor and Security Company

Effective, highly efficient, and secure are helpful aspects to performing business in 2020. And one that checks off all of the boxes is biometric sensors.

Biometric sensors are generally used to gather individuals' biological characteristics such as fingerprints, voice recognition, iris identification, facial images, and so on. Any behavioral or psychological characteristics will do the trick in ensuring that the biometric sensor readily identifies and verifies security and authenticity.

The biometrics market, which is 100 percent automated, is worth more than $16 billion and even projected to see a CAGE of approximately 35.5 percent from 2020-2025. However, there are both advantages and disadvantages that this system has. Here are the benefits and drawbacks of Biometric Security:

Pros

- Allows physical access to internal resources, buildings as well as computer systems without the risk of any security breach. It also strengthens existing security systems that utilize password-only measures.
- Automated calculation of employee hours minimizes manual and paper tracking systems that save companies both time and money.

Cons

- Initial set-up costs are significant
- Limited privacy for users
- There is still a risk of hackers or data breaches
- 8. DDoS Cyber Attack Prevention Security Company

DDoS (denial of service) attack is a desperately harmful or malicious endeavor designed to disrupt the traffic to your network or a computer server. The primary goal of a DDoS attack is to ensure your online service remains unavailable to your customers.

This comes about by flooding your service or network with lots of bogus requests, thereby impeding legitimate traffic from accessing your website. As you will agree, this is not nice and can even be very disruptive for business owners or startups.

DDoS attacks can be very costly to root, which will cost the company a lot of money to repair the damage and cost the firm its potential customers. The only way to stop these trouble-makers in their tracks is by hiring a DDoS cyber-attack prevention security company.

Research has shown that the DDoS protection and mitigation market is expected to reach up to $9.10 billion by 2025. And it is projected to have a CAGR of 24.9 percent from 2020 to 2025, which tells you that the perfect time to enter the industry is now.

The number of attacks keeps growing steadily, making more individuals and business owners proactively enlist the professional service and assistance of DDoS security companies. These security companies handle the following:

- Establish security infrastructure components

- Stop DDoS attacks within minutes, thereby minimizing any or all disruption to your businesses.

- Enhanced flexibility that blends third-party and in-house resources like dedicated and cloud server hosting

- Cleans up all the mess and quickly reroutes all legitimate traffic to your network.

9. Stem Cell Therapy

The revenue-generating potential of stem cell therapy is so enormous that it is somewhat surprising all the big boys are not in this industry.

Experts have predicted that stem cell therapy will continuously experience a massive growth with a CAGR of 27.99 percent over the next ten years. And the best part is that entrepreneurs without a scientific or medical background can reap the massive and growing income potential.

There are more than a few ways you can tap into this growing market. For instance, you can start a testing lab, a stem cell bank, or even use stem cells in health and beauty products. Or you may opt to invest heavily into any of these options stated below:

- Invest in stem cell stocks
- Become an affiliate or distributor for dedicated websites
- Open a 'for profit' stem cell unit or clinic or opt for the mobile route in order to minimize costs.

10. Senior At-Home Care

It always matters a lot to ensure your loved ones retain their independence and comfort at all times. This will help to bypass concerns about the level of compassion and care your family member will receive.

For seniors who are still functional, at-home seniors are the best alternative for them as nursing home costs rise significantly high while homes are getting even more crowded these days. Trained staff and service providers assist seniors with appointments, medication as well as other household duties or activity. They are also highly skilled in handling different types of equipment a senior may require at any time of the day.

Hiring a home health assistant or aide is something that many families are willing to do because it saves them tons of money, especially after carrying out cost comparisons. Any business model that supports families of all backgrounds and situations is one worth investing in.

According to recent statistics, by 2030, one out of every 5 Americans will be 65 years or older, which opens a myriad of opportunities for senior at-home care businesses such as:

- Meal prep
- House cleaning and errands
- Non-medical in-home care
- Companion
- Personal care assistance
- Nutrition and fitness consulting
- Medical claims assistance
- Money management and financial planning
- Property management

You can maximize your earning potential when you launch this future business idea.

Chapter Four

Top 20 Best Future Business Ideas for 2020-2030 (Part II)

Continuing from where the last chapter ended...

11. Asteroid Mining

Do you know that precious material like silver, gold, diamonds, and platinum are found all over space? Space travel is still developing and is expected to become even more advanced. One of the first issues that corporations will address will have to do with mining asteroid for precious minerals like diamond and gold.

This is a serious and major undertaking that may not even be feasible until 2030. However, it is worth investing in, and many big companies are presently and extremely focused on this.

Research has shown that even a tiny section of space could be worth more than double the Earth's entire wealth. This means that the first set of individuals who manage to get a spacecraft to a resource-loaded asteroid could quickly become the world's wealthiest people.

Investing in asteroid mining could be capital-intensive as you may need to create robots and drones that will aid in drilling as well as mining asteroids. Whichever way you see it, this is an industry with a lot of incredible potentials and, of course, for people who are daring enough to try the impossible.

12. eCommerce

The world has virtually moved online, changing almost everything from the way things are purchased to delivery at your doorstep. Businesses that are not taking a leaf from the eCommerce industry run the risk of getting left behind.

This year alone, it has an estimated that consumers in the United States will spend more than $709 billion on eCommerce, representing a growth rate of 18 percent. This is slated to hit up to $4.9 trillion by 2021.

One thing is sure: eCommerce is the retail market tomorrow. And what makes eCommerce unique is that you do not even have to own or make the products you sell. All that you need to do is to utilize another aspect of eCommerce known as Dropshipping.

You can also choose to be an affiliate, a system of selling products which is explained later on. The truth is that the financial advantages of running an eCommerce business are staggering. Take a look at the following eCommerce highlights:

- Higher ROIs

- Elevated business reach

- Easy to track

- More search engine traffic

- Logistically solid

- Flexible, scalable, and profitable

- Automated product delivery systems

There is no better period to get online than now because, by 2030, the majority of shopping will be conducted online, i.e., digitally. Consumers will only use brick and mortar establishments as an experience. And such businesses will need to make considerable changes such as price reductions and specialization if they hope to stay in the game extensively.

13. Wallet Payment Solution

Wallet payment solutions have been somewhat slow to catch on in the U.S.A. Nevertheless, it is a market that is on its way to becoming a national corporation.

Wallet payment has to do with monetary transactions made with a virtual or digital wallet via a software program. It securely stores people's payment details and ensures purchases are super-easy.

This money-making concept is somewhat unknown in the United States because most people living in the country possess credit and debit cards, which are convenient, simple, and trusted means of payment.

Nevertheless, wallet payment solutions are taking some countries – such as China and India – by storm. Therefore, it is merely a question of time before the trend will take hold in the U.S. as well as other parts of the globe. It is currently projected to be worth an estimated and whopping $130 billion by the end of 2020.

This market has some established and hefty competition like Masterpass, ApplePay, and Chase Pay. However, it is just proof that there is a lot of money to be made in this industry since these brands are players there.

You can secure profitability in this industry that will soon change the entire trajectory of the world's future within a short time.

14. Virtual Interior Design Consulting

Interior design is all about placement and visuals, as well as the ability to transform a space into a comfortable and scenic sanctuary for clients.

The advent and rise of technology have made it possible for enthusiasts to launch an interior design business and run it from the sanctuary of their homes with nothing but a laptop, camera gear, tablet, software, and social media.

You will see the exterior and interior of a client's office space or property via the lens of your camera. Then, the next thing that you should do is to create stunning mockups for your clients, send them over, and consult regarding the next step to take.

As you well know, the marketing of your new remote interior design and consulting business will depend significantly on social media, your official website as well as getting in touch with your current connections within your network while working hard to create new ones.

15. Affiliate Marketing

Affiliate Marketing involves the promotion of someone else's products – using any means at your disposal – that you love or have tried and tested. And if someone purchases that product based on your promotion efforts and testimonials, you will receive a commission.

This is an online marketing model that you can leverage without doing the tough job of creating the product, handling customer complaints or support, and so on.

This is a business model that works incredibly well that up to 81 percent of businesses are currently taking advantage of this model in one way or the other. And if you set things up the right way, you can be making money passively or in your sleep for many years to come as long as your niche site remains live on the web.

16. IT Service and Support

The face of the corporate world will eventually be digital since more and more businesses, and individuals will continue to rely even more heavily on the internet as well as social media platforms. There will be a proliferation of software and hardware to contend favorably with this immense growth.

These vital tools will ultimately generate an influx in demand for both IT service and support enterprises. The projected growth rate for IT services is up to 22 percent in 2020 alone. Software development and other facets are seeing upwards of 32 percent growth rate, making it one of the best future business ideas to explore today.

Many business and individuals from around the world will need help with setup and maintenance and troubleshooting issues. This is because the most of the population in the United States is astonishingly clueless when it comes to tech stuff.

Remarkable advancements in technology around Cloud computing, Blockchain, AI, and even elevated automation will leave some of the most tech-savvy individuals and organizations seeking professional assistance. This is where you will come in as the messiah, especially if you love tech stuff or prefer to be called a tech nerd.

The options within the IT service and support niche are numerous, and this includes:

- IT Managers
- Database Admins
- Product Manager
- Software Inventory
- Blockchain Engineer
- Cloud Architect
- DevOps Designer
- Artificial Intelligence Engineer of AI Engineer

This is just a small section of an extensive list that you can explore to your satisfaction.

17. VR Live Events

Is there an annual conference that you can't make or want to enjoy your favorite band while still on tour? Do you even know that you can get a ticket for those events and experience them as if you were there in the flesh from your study or living room?

This is made possible thanks to VR, which helps individuals worldwide to readily access live events, helping the hosts generate mouth-watering and untold revenue.

At present, the revenue for virtual events is up to $78 billion, and projections currently suggest that this number will significantly grow to a breathtaking $774 billion by 2030.

Believe it or not, everything from conferences and exhibitions to music concerts is headed in the direction of virtual implementation. This implies that there won't be a limit to the sale of tickets based on the availability of space as it will now be possible to sell hundreds of millions of tickets to in-person and virtual spectators.

The adoption of VR for the modern world was not expected to take off as it did, but the scourge of the pandemic saw to it. The industry has been predicted to witness an unbelievable CAGR of 33.47 percent, which speaks volumes about its profitability for businesses in the space.

As it stands, the projected growth rate will even be much higher than this.

18. Virtual Event Planning Platform

Event planning has now taken on a new look and is presently leaning even more on online and virtual affairs.

Video streaming services have successfully eliminated geographical constraints, thereby allowing event planners to host exceptional virtual events to remote audiences. Embracing this virtual event to maintain cash flow and profitability is the best way for event planners to stay in business in these modern times.

To execute stellar events online, the following crucial fundamentals must be in place:

- Pick your platform
- Understand the needs as well as the expectations of your audience
- Develop or create your format and how you intend to make your event unique
- Determine the venue, day, and time

- Choose an MC or host that can captivate your audience and is highly entertaining.

- Always keep it simple, short, and to the point.

Event planners provide both a service and an experience. This is a business model that will continue to generate substantial profits with some creativity and the right infrastructure, as well as the willingness to shift to online solutions.

19. Tele and Video Conferencing

The pandemic has touched all aspects of the economy, especially face-to-face interactions and regular office work. It has resulted in the significant adoption of teleconferencing and video conferencing, and businesses like Zoom has climbed up Forbes' list, thanks to massive signups and subscriptions from multi-national organizations. The virtual meetings hosted by Zoom over the past few months cannot be quantified.

This can only mean one thing: video conferencing and teleconferencing are the new norms on how to conduct business transactions. From business communication and networking, teleconferencing provides individuals and associates worldwide the opportunity and ability to maintain highly productive or effective communication even amid the global pandemic.

The education industry has also taken a hit and has adopted teleconferencing and video conferencing as the best way to overcome the throes of COVID-19.

What if you had foreseen this circumstance and bought shares or even owned at least one of these teleconferencing and video conferencing conglomerates? That would have been cool, isn't it? Well, it is not too late because this business venture still has a futuristic appeal.

According to a well-researched publication, teleconferencing and video conferencing have been projected to see a growth rate of approximately 9.8 percent from 2020-2026. And it will purportedly reach a market value of more than $6 billion in the United States of America alone. This is too huge a pie to pass up, especially if you want to get in on the action in this growing industry that is reaching record highs and breaking barriers left, right, and center.

Teleconferencing, as well as video conferencing, efficiently delivers alternate options in order to maintain productivity, efficiency, and personalization.

20. eSports

eSports offer a gamer's paradise with the competitive edge of live competitions. Organized tournaments in several sports –via video games – have started taking on a digital presence, as well as a lot of people around the world are taking notice.

And with the way the popularity of eSports is growing, it is presently estimated that viewership will see a CAGR of 9 percent from 2020-2023, and will purportedly fetch revenues that is more than 4646 million by the end of that stipulated time frame.

Game enthusiasts love the social component of eSports, and you will agree that we are a highly competitive bunch in any field. Live streaming, and social media platforms, are generally the driving forces behind the remarkable growth of this industry with no sign of slowing down.

And you can take a slice of this cake by jumping in on the action today. You can launch an eSports platform of your own as long as you are ready to adhere to the following recommendations:

- Choose your ideal target market and geographical area.
- Hone down the niche; pick one popular sport that you love and get after it.
- Organize your team and don't forget to include branding
- Put your infrastructure in place with the appropriate hardware. This should include a user-friendly eSports website.
- Secure sponsorships in order to fund this endeavor to enable you to compete at an elevated position.
- Remember to pick a location and aggressively promote your team.
- Fans, as well as additional recruitment options, is a must.

There is no doubt that eSports is presently revolutionizing virtual, competitive gaming and is considered one of the best future business ideas to adopt for 2020-2030. You can conduct in-depth research to ascertain what it takes to be incredibly successful in this 21st-century business.

In the next two chapters, we will be taking a look at Facebook Marketing and YouTube Marketing. Implementing these marketing strategies incredibly well has the potential of generating passive income for you.

Chapter Six

Facebook Marketing

In the first few years of social media networking, MySpace was the big boy. Between 2003 and 2006, it grew extraordinarily to 100 million users, and by June 2006, the website was even more visited than Google. Then came Facebook.

By 2008, Facebook had dramatically surpassed MySpace in global users and U.S. users about a year later. And as MySpace severely declined (it plummeted to about 25 million users as of June 2012), some businesses started to wonder about making significant advertising investments in Facebook. They feared it might also be displaced as MySpace was. But that was not the case.

In fact, globally, it's the biggest social media platform, with over 2.27 billion active users and almost 1.5 billion of whom are very active each day.

You will still find the best marketing opportunities on the world's biggest social network, and that is not going to change anytime soon. Spending time learning Facebook marketing is defintely worth the investment.

You are about to discover the basics or fundamentals of how to use Facebook to your utmost advantage. The book targets beginners or neophytes who want an introduction to marketing their numerous businesses on the world's #1 social media network.

What is Facebook marketing?

Facebook marketing refers to the creation—and active usage— of a Facebook page as a channel for communication, maintaining contact with and also attracting numerous users or potential clients. Facebook actively provides for this as it allows users to create individual profiles or business pages for organizations, firms, or any group attempting to develop a fan base for a product, service, or brand.

Who Can Utilize Facebook Marketing?

Every business should be using Facebook. It is as crucial as having a business website page—and much easier to create. Whether you represent an NGO or big brand or even a small startup that employs a handful of people, you can be sure that some portion of your customers is on Facebook. Commonly, Facebook marketing is used by:

- Brands. Electronics, food, home goods, and restaurants—nearly any kind of brand can be seriously promoted on Facebook, turning passive users or customers into active and raving fans who follow news of promotions and developments and share with friends on the platform.

- Personalities. Celebrities, musicians, authors, syndicated columnists—anybody who makes their legitimate money by being known- want to be known by as many individuals as possible on Facebook.

- Local businesses. Whether a business is a franchise of a larger company or family-owned, a Facebook Page can be used to transform a local customer base into a raving fan base that will frequently visit your store.

- Non-profit organizations. Charities, public service campaigns, and political groups can all leverage the natural sharing capabilities of Facebook.

Is your audience on Facebook?

Is your audience even on Facebook? The answer is, in all probability.

The most recent data shows that every age uses at least one social media network site, with younger users with higher percentages.

Moreover, both men and women use social media in approximately equal numbers.

And when it comes to which social media network many people use, Facebook dominates the list. As of January 2018, 68 percent of Americans used Facebook, with Instagram in distant second place with 35 percent.

Put differently, no matter what age group you are targeting, there will be more than enough of such users on Facebook.

Here's how to get little things set up and start promoting your products or services through Facebook;

Market with Facebook Pages

The first Facebook marketing tool for brands is Facebook Pages. Like a personal Facebook profile, a Page is the virtual hub of information for your brand, be it an organization, service, product, or even a celebrity or expert.

Facebook users can always "Like" a page they are interested in and also "Follow" it, which means they will automatically start receiving updates from that particular Page in their news feed.

But to see the posts every time they put up online, you need to click the option to view posts first. Otherwise, it is highly likely you won't see the updates because Facebook wants Pages to readily boost posts (by paying) for more visibility and reach.

So when you get Facebook users to like your Page, it is often considered a good idea to recommend they follow you so that they can see your posts first. It will save you lots of your hard-earned money if you do not have to boost posts as often or often.

There are a few major differences to take note of between Facebook Pages and Facebook Profiles. Connecting with someone as a personal profile will require both of you to confirm the friendship request.

When you have a Page, Facebook users can 'Like' and 'Follow' without your approval.

Another significant difference is that there are practically no limits to the number of users that can 'Like' your Facebook Page. If you have a personal/profile account, you cannot have more than 5,000 friends. But a Facebook Page can have thousands or even millions of people who 'like' it.

The best part of Pages is that they are free and very easy to set up. You can build a new Page in the next 15 minutes and make it look as professional as that of a Fortune 500 company.

The only downside is that—they can be tough to get off the ground. Unless you are a celebrity or notable brands like BMW or Coke, it takes a lot of work to get more people to 'like' your Page.

But if you are going to start with this, you will need to set up a professional page. Here is how to go about it:

How to set up the Ideal Facebook Page

It is quite unfortunate that many organizations do not use Facebook Pages to their full potential. Worse, some brands even use them very poorly and actually hurt their credibility.

The following guidelines will help you avoid making those silly mistakes;

Good Profile photo and cover image

Your profile photo should be your brand logo. The cover image, however, is a different story. This is because it is really up to you to decide what to put here. Some brands use photos of employees, while others use artwork and put their contact information in the cover image. M&Ms, for instance, does a great job blending their logo, characters, and product into their photos.

-Pick and use a photo that will enhance your Page and catch the attention of your visitors.

-The "About" section

The "About" section is placed immediately below your company logo. This is your best chance to tell anyone coming to your Page what your business does. It is short, so do not try to fit everything in. In the full 'About' section, make sure to add more details.

Explain what your organization or brand does, why you are unique, along with other interesting facts. Take your time to write it for your Facebook audience.

If you have a brick and mortar business, you can add a few more features like hours and locations. Remember to keep it as friendly as you can and as informal as possible. A casual tone works best on Facebook.

-Post valuable info on your timeline

What you post to your timeline will show up in the news feeds of everyone who has "Liked" your Page, the same way it does when you post something to your personal profile.

So, make sure whatever you are posting is incredibly useful to your fans. Do not post continuous updates about the same thing. And do not post too often as this action may clog the news feeds of your fans.

Major brands like Apple usually post things they know will be very interesting to their fans, like product announcements or unique video ads.

Quick ideas for the type of information you should post to your wall include:

- New product announcements
- Links to articles related to your industry or company
- Links to your blog posts
- Links to useful online tools that your fans might find useful
- Coupon codes for followers to save on your products

Customized videos that will appeal to your target audience – You can use InVideo to make impactful and high-quality videos for Facebook

Again, make sure that your posts are interesting or helpful. Do not post more than a few times each day unless there is a special event going on.

One of the surest and dumbest ways to lose your followers is spam. If you don't do anything other than sending promotional blurbs about your brand without first of all add anything of value, you are going to have a tough time getting fans.

Before you post any update on your Facebook Page, ask yourself if it honestly adds value to the conversation.

Study your stats and results

Facebook Insights offers some excellent analytics for pages. Pay close attention to it. If you notice a big surge in fans (or even a significant drop off), take a look at what you may have posted recently to see if you can figure out a reason for the trend.

Then, start posting more of that kind of content (or less, if you're losing fans).

Using groups, the marketplace, and jobs

Over the last few years, Facebook has created several new features for different types of pages. Here is how to use them to each one to promote your company or brand.

How to Market with Facebook Groups

Facebook has had groups for some time. But they recently allow users to create brand-based groups associated with your Page.

First, you will need a Facebook Page for your brand. Then you can create a dedicated group to go with that Page. This allows you to have a little more control over the Facebook group since you can attach your company to it.

Facebook groups are very similar to dedicated discussion forums but with additional features that pages and profiles have (like a timeline). You can create groups that are related to your industry or product offerings in order to reach out to prospective customers.

The beautiful thing about Facebook Groups is that they're free, like Pages. They also have high levels of engagement. But the main downside is that they can be incredibly time-consuming.

To manage a Page, you may only need to check it once a day (or even less) to post something helpful and reply to comments.

With a Group, you'll want to monitor discussions continually, post relevant questions, and manage the members—perhaps several times a day.

How to Market Using Facebook Marketplace

If you have some products to sell, Facebook Marketplace might be the game-changer for you. It is very similar to Craigslist but built directly into the Facebook ecosystem.

Facebook's relatively newer feature is still revising, but it has enormous potential for eCommerce retailers as well as other types of product-based businesses.

When you list such products, they become searchable across Facebook, and other users can find them.

How to use Facebook Jobs

Finally, you can post jobs to Facebook. This is a newer feature, which was launched in the last few years or so.

Of course, this is not typical marketing like most people use on Facebook, but it can be beneficial if you are looking to hire someone.

Targeted Advertising

Facebook offers a highly targeted advertising platform.

You can create ads targeted that are specific to geographic areas, education levels, ages, and even the types of mobile devices used for browsing. Facebook also lets users hide ads that they do not like and "Like" a page right underneath an advertisement.

Because Facebook gathers a lot of demographic information about its users, the platform has one of the best and highly targeted ad programs online. You can target Facebook users based on virtually anything you might find in their profiles and track your success with every segment.

(It is also their most controversial feature, and one that has gotten them into some trouble recently. But let's set that aside in the meantime and focus on using these tools.)

Adverts can be run on a per-click or per-impression basis. Facebook shows marketers what bids are for ads that are similar to yours so that you know if your bid is in conformity with others within your industry. You can even set daily limits, so there is no risk of blowing your budget.

The advantage is that Facebook ads are compelling, and they are more likely to succeed than groups or pages since users can choose who sees the ads.

The downside is the cost. It is easy to run lots of Facebook ads without making anything back, so keep track of your budget.

Types of Facebook Ads

There are several ad sub-types you can choose from.

These include offers, video, leads, canvas, carousel, and many other types. Each one has a particular advantage and can be useful depending on the particular type of marketing you are embarking on.

One of the best methods to help you decide on the type of advert to run is to take a look at what your competitors are doing. You can go to the "Info and Ads" tab on any company page, and you can see what ads are active.

(You can also change the country if you like to see promotions in other regions.)

To create a new ad campaign, you will need to be the administrator of a page. From there, you can go into the Ad Manager.

It is a very complicated tool, but there is no need to start with all features

You should get used to the most important metrics and buttons for your brand and then build from there. You can always learn more a little later when you have used it for some time.

Powerful Targeting Options

Facebook has some of the most powerful, super-targeting tools of any online advertising program. You can target by anything on a user's profile. You might start with the location. You can specify the city, zip code, county, or even state.

This works incredibly well for local businesses. You can choose basic demographics, including age, relationship status, workplace, education (including both major and years of attendance), birthday, and much more.

You can target ads to Facebook users who have recently moved. So, if you own a gym in Hollywood and want to find all the individuals who recently moved to the neighborhood, you can easily target your ads and copy them.

You also can target users based on their interests. Say, for example, you have a new or unique product that is aimed at Cricket fans. You could enter Cricket in the 'Interests' field.

Or, maybe you have written a book, and you are sure that people who like another book in your genre will love yours. Enter the title of the book under 'Interests,' and you will specifically target only those users.

You can also target a private list of users. If you have an email list of of users that you want to target, you can easily use Facebook's Ads Manager to target those people.

Therefore, if you run a SaaS - Software as a service - business and have at least 200 people on your "prospect list," you can use their specific email addresses to target them with ads on Facebook.

Customize Your Ads

The other significant advantage of tightly-targeted ads is that you can create different or several ads for different demographic groups. Highly-targeted ads are going to garner much better results.

If you are targeting baseball fans, you might create individual ads for different popular teams. You could have one ad aimed explicitly at Cubs fans, one at Yankees fans, and another at Red Sox fans.

Then, you could have only those ads shown only to people who have previously indicated in their 'Interests' that they are raving fans of those baseball teams.

Or, let's say you have targeted people based on their love of a particular book, e.g., Harry Potter. You could mention that book in the advert itself in order to make it much more likely to catch their attention. Create different ads for different books in the genre and target accordingly.

Wrapping Up

Facebook isn't only powerful, but it's also flexible. No matter what type of establishment or organization you run, the social media platform has different marketing options to tailor your marketing efforts in order to fit your company, your budget, as well as your time constraints.

Yes, it can take a bit of time to get to know all of its features, but it's worth it. Facebook continues growing at a rapid pace, and every day it becomes a more indispensable part of social media marketing.

If Facebook is not presently part of your marketing campaign, it should be. Therefore, set aside some time to tinker around, launch a few test campaigns in order to see what happens.

Chapter Seven

YouTube Marketing

YouTube is a social media platform where modern video culture was born. It has set trends and forms the demand for new video formats.

YouTube has given brands unprecedented opportunities to promote their products or services, create an image, and always keep up with the numerous requests of their target audiences.

Video content is presently ahead of other forms of advertising as outlined below:

- 59 percent of managers would rather watch a video than read a text;

- 64 percent of users are much more likely to purchase a product or service after watching a video about it;

- Most users stay on a page with the video almost 90 percent longer than on the page without it;

- Posts on social media networks with videos have 48 percent more views.

These figures suggest that creating original videos is not enough. The quality and content are what really matter. You need to develop an innovative video marketing strategy to capture the market.

In this chapter, the following shall be considered:

- Why YouTube marketing is a must-have for your marketing strategy
- How to create a highly successful YouTube marketing strategy in 2020
- The YouTube trends that will emerge
- The YouTube video formats you should focus on in the upcoming year.
- Video Content as a cutting-edge YouTube Marketing Strategy Foundation

Content marketing is something akin to a magic pill for many organizations. To present a product or service and make a prospective consumer want to buy it, a seller should totally influence the target audience. Podcasts, infographics, courses, texts, personal brand, etc. – i.e., everything is used.

But there is one promotion direction that completely overshadows the rest – and that is video marketing.

Video is the foundation of the YouTube marketing strategy, and here is how it becomes a robust tool of influence:

- Video easily simplifies user interaction with relevant information. Unlike texts or articles, videos don't force people to strain themselves to read.
- You can start the video and comprehend the information in the background.
- Videos combine both visual and sound effects to evoke emotions quickly and don't leave a user feeling somewhat indifferent.
- Video content is very easy to interact with – from smartphones, anytime and anywhere.

The most popular convenient platform for uploading and watching videos these days is YouTube, the third most-visited site after Google and Facebook. Up to 400 minutes of video are uploaded to YouTube every minute, and over 1 billion hours are viewed daily.

YouTube was initially designed for entertainment purposes, but today, it has grown significantly and is used for business promotion.

In 2019, almost 63 percent of brands used YouTube as a platform for the development of their business.

But how to make your compelling YouTube marketing strategy a real lead-generation machine in 2020 and beyond? At least, you should start applying the following YouTube trends and video formats.

YouTube Video Formats and Trends that You Must Use in 2020

A well-thought-out and carefully-planned YouTube marketing strategy should be based on the users' preferences, interests, and needs. Therefore, your task is to transform the commercial message into useful material, presented in one of the following YouTube formats:

- YouTube Live;
- Unboxing video;
- "How to" guides;
- Users decide;

- Videos around a particular routine;

- Trendy themes;

- 360-degree content;

- YouTube ads;

- Visual storytelling;

- YouTube as a search engine.

YouTube Live

This user interaction format is one of the most efficient marketing methods as it allows the viewer to interact with the speaker in real-time mode. The YouTube Live function has gradually replaced conventional, already-recorded videos; people spend eight times more time watching live videos on YouTube than watching ready-made or recorded videos.

Those who launch live broadcasts allow prospective consumers to influence the content: ask questions, clarify, and in such a way to feel more significant and valuable.

If you have never run YouTube live broadcasts before, it's high time you mastered this method.

Unboxing videos

Before making a purchase, eighty percent of users first watch a video tutorial or look for answers to their questions on YouTube. The platform has become a kind of unique search engine system where users can find answers to each of their requests. And how does YouTube affect users' buying experience? Several types of YouTube videos serve this particular purpose almost all at once:

Unpacking;

Real-time shopping;

Answers to questions – where and how to purchase a product.

Consumers choose brands when they feel some emotional connection. Thus, unboxing videos, which is one of the hottest YouTube trends, allows organizations to establish a positive experience with prospective clients and buyers. Video content is the most promising and shortest path to fall in mutual love with potential and existing customers.

A lovely idea is to address some influential YouTube bloggers to advertise your product through the unboxing video.

Users decide

One of the most promising trends you should add to your YouTube marketing strategy in 2020 and beyond is asking users for help. You can ask the viewers or subscribers what topic to deal with in the next video and their real interests.

For this, conduct surveys and polls, and urge users to leave their valued opinions in the comment section. All these will help you understand your subscribers' preferences and record great videos based on them. Thus, they are far more likely to achieve a well-defined business goal.

Videos around the routine

This type of video shows how celebrities and bloggers (or you) start their day, how they get super ready for bed at the end of the day, and so on. A similar format is in demand among YouTube subscribers. It helps them to efficiently organize the same daily tasks (morning coffee, makeup removal, house cleaning, training in the gym, etc.).

Plus, daily-actions-videos bring brands/bloggers closer to subscribers due to showing the stuff they have in common with users.

360-degree Content

YouTube video formats with 360-degree Content provide incredible immersion as well as unforgettable experiences for viewers. Users appear to be transferred to the picture they see, thereby reducing the distance between them and a product/brand.

360-Degree Content is one of the most efficient ways to present the product in detail and motivate buyers to purchase it. This transforms it into a lead-generation machine, especially when used in Facebook video ads.

YouTube Ads

Advertising on television is becoming less popular and profitable; it is replaced by advertising on YouTube. Over 75 percent of adults watch videos YouTube in prime time, which ultimately shortens the brands' reach for users. You can readily achieve high lead-generation results if you always implement the latest YouTube trends when running mobile advertising.

Visual storytelling

Users always want to be very close to the favorite celebrities and brands, so you should create videos that provide that feeling of proximity. Such videos may document events or personal stories, for example.

You can easily record amateur videos and upload one episode a week to make users eager for the next portion. This really boosts user engagement as well as retention. Try a visual storytelling technique in order to bring your brand closer to the target audience.

Conclusion

To wrap up, always beware when someone tells you there is no work involved in passive income. If passive income is your goal, you have to perform your due diligence, and that is work. Whatever investments you make requires constant management and checking up on the industries' progress where your investments are. And that, my dear friend, is work, too!

However, the good news is that both management and research will be a part-time endeavor. And you can do this work anywhere you are in the world.

Above all, do not forget to have fun as you research and implement the passive income plans that will enable you to live your dreams to the fullest. Making money every day, every week, and every month is fun, and testing your hands on the two most popular marketing strategies outlined in this book is fun as well.

So, go out there, implement what you have studied in this book, and take action!